GRAVE
DELIGHTS

GRAVE DELIGHTS

N'GADIE ROBERTS

A catalogue record for this
work is available from the
National Library of Australia

www.ngadieroberts.com
Roberts, N'Gadie (author)
Signal, Wilma (illustrator)
Grave Delights
ISBN 978-1-922629-89-0
Poetry

Typeset Baskerville URW 11/15

Edited by Teneal Zuvela.
Cover and book design by Green Hill Publishing

To my family, for all your love and sacrifice. To my friends, readers, and mentors for your endless support. Thank you for joining me on this journey.

"The heart is deceitful above all things and beyond cure. Who can understand it?" Jeremiah 17:9

CONTENTS

CONTENTS

CONTENTS

CONTENTS

PART I

MIDNIGHT
STORYTELLERS

Sweet Lavender

My sweet Lavender.
The last time I saw her was in the forest,
running to meet
The Harvest Man.
Angelic braids trailed down her back
swaying to the song of the wind.
I waited for her to look back
one last time. She didn't,
she ran until her silhouette
dissolved into the moonlight.

Villagers
found her body the next morning,
stiff as a pan-body.
"Na juju, na witch, na debul – so so kongossa."

I should have followed her,
I should have told her
that I wanted her.

~

Last night
I went to a place called mourning,
where the eyelids of the sea
washed my feet. I saw her again;
my sweet Lavender, her face
a faraway sunrise.

My wife often asks me
why I'm quiet at night.
I say it's nothing.
She thinks I'm worried about the IVF.
She knows not of the old albatross
around my neck.

"I like the name Caden if it's a boy."

How do I tell her
that I'm haunted by memories
of another woman — of my sister,
my sweet Lavender? And that she died
on her way to take care of
the child
I put inside her.

LUNA LAGOON

The moon is the oldest philosopher
all things hath he seen.
But where does he go
when man wakes from dream?

Some say he enters
the bleeding loins of hell
where wry wayward widows
and dragons doth dwell.

Others say he sleeps
with stars during day
pleasuring himself,
galaxies away.

The moon is the oldest sorcerer,
see how he sways the tides!
But where does he go
when man opens eyes?

Some say he ventures
a seaward direction
seeking his pale,
banal reflection.

I say he hides
in the lonesome lagoon
where another one turned
late last June.

The moon is the oldest watcher
all waves hath he seen
including the sound
of a werewolf's scream.

WELL FED

I like to feed
seabirds
in winter;
when the air is stagnant
and no one is watching.

It's a habit I've had since I was nine
a meticulous one, this habit of mine.

I like to feed seabirds
in winter
to the hungry wolf inside of me.

Sunset, I glimpse their spirits
fluttering softly across the sea.

Midnight, I hide their bones
down
in the lighthouse
down
by the sea.

TRAVELLER'S QUEST

They left the fire
and the dying light
in search of cold, grey lands
but all they found
was an eternally setting sun.

Jewels for the Hunter

They arrived on horseback that night,
carrying a sack full
of tea leaves and royal rubies.
Nuns from the East
running from the chains
of unholy couplings.

I offered them food,
I offered them water
but all they wanted was rest.

Moonbeams exposed aging blood
on bitter palms.

I offered them blankets,
I offered them tents; but
all they wanted was rest.
~

News anchors
drown us in stories; missing horse riders,
gone without a trace. The words
illegal immigrants are expelled like faeces
on hallowed ground. The case is assigned to my
department
but certainly
bodies won't be found.

No heart, no kidney,
no precious jewels.

I ensured that I was careful.
I wolfed the flesh
and buried their bones
deep in the womb
of an evergreen forest.

DAUGHTERS OF THE MOON

Here in Aegon,
the leaves do not rustle
the flowers do not bloom
and the dead, never buried.
Instead, bodies
are carried
into waters
embracing the town's coastline.

It begins:
a shipwreck, hours proceeding dawn
three girls, one song
one sailor, one storm.

Primordial caves beckon to the sailor. They echo with
voices purple,
like plums.

Lamps made of kerosene, feminine fingers fumbling.
Ripe curves
stale youth –
a combustible mix.

Kisses shared, offering prepared.
Rocks raised, up
down, hacking, cracking, smashing
cracking.

The ivory sand begins to blush
and order is restored.

Here in Aegon,
the leaves do not rustle
the flowers do not bloom
but The Ferryman is rich
throughout a full moon.

VOYAGER

Freedom is a mystic voyage
we must embark on.
A journey
that swallows us
into the oesophagus
of aching dreams,
until we reach
the belly of hope.

THE SMILE OF A STRANGER

Follow me into the forest, you must!
We'll gather fresh plum,
and taste running rum.

See fairy floss bloom
from baobab trees,

suck succulent sweets
as long as you please!

Delve deep inside,
don't be afraid!

The locals are having
their annual parade.

They'll sing
and sway
and prance
and pray
and cheer
for the new found
visitors here!

They'll dress you in gold,
and fatten you up

then sacrifice you
for a yield of crop!

You'll burn and turn and
sizzle with rage
all the while burning alive in a cage.

Follow me
into the forest
you must,

I'm wearing a smile you sightseers trust.

COUNTRY YEARNING

She wanted a quiet life of
creeks and cows,
salt dishes, and children
in the water, drowning
in laughter.

MORNING GOWNS AND MANDARINS

The whiff of maple syrup calls in the day as
we sit by the breakfast table
outside,
surrounded by citrus trees,
some yellow, some green.

"Have some lemon curd with these pancakes," you insist.

I shake my head.

Crinkles form on the sides of your eyes.
They squeeze out a smile. "It's your recipe; do you
remember it?"

I shake my head again. Layered throbs numb my temples.

"Rose water relieves headaches," you say.

This makes me laugh.
I've never believed in your golden remedies,
though you offer them to me like silver coins.

"I'm serious, these doctors don't know everything."

I sigh. *But it's a brain tumour, mama. I know it's hard to accept, but your rose water remedies aren't going to cut it.*

LOCKDOWN

Hospital rooms
are closed like confessionals.
Behind their curtains
men grapple with affliction.

"Forgive me doctor, for I have sinned.
It has been a year since my last visit.
I am guilty
of congregating in crowds,
not washing my hands clean."

But the doctor can offer
no absolution
no cure for their affliction.
This is mortality.

MAMI WATA

I used to visit her in
her cottage by the sea.
My grandmother.
She spun silky stories
of a creature some had seen
and one that swam in streams.

It spoke in storms,
a spirit of the ages
cast away
into sunken seas.

Seal coat
night eyes,
ancient foe in amorous disguise. Hands, hands
the colour of mahogany,
and palms
palms as white as the shells on the shore.

I never saw that creature on the rocks
but I could always feel it;
dwelling
in the crevices of my memory.

BENEATH THE JAZZY SKY

Dusk arrives at his usual hour.
Tonight, he's wearing stormy blue trousers
and a marigold coat woven with winds.

The coat contains three pockets, inside
pearls of rain. I watch
as he ever so slowly, takes them out and
pitter-patter
pitter-patter
scatters them
along the city skyline.

OLD LOVER'S DEN

I wanted to start anew
but this place
it's bathed in memories of you
and I'm having a hard time
bidding them
adieu.

TEQUILA MOCKINGBIRD

The night breathed fresh fog
on her bedroom window
masking
her intruder's silhouette.

Screams. Shots. Silence.

The city carried on.
At midnight she mumbles:

Please remember
your key next time
but thanks for bringing
the tequila and lime.

More shots.

HOUSE OF GHOSTS

I have to go
to the house of ghosts.
Please do not wait for me;
you have your own giants to fight.

MY GRANDMOTHER

Along the beach I amble,
listening to your parables;

sacred daughters of the moon,
a king who lost his pantaloons.

High. Euphoric sighs. Turquoise
turns to teal; oceans are nothing but divine opium
and I am addicted.
Cloying winds come and go, like the men who discard me
at their leisure.

But your stories, in them I find pleasure. This one is new:

"It begins
a shipwreck, in the hours proceeding dawn
three girls, one song
one sailor, one storm."

Your words roll out;
a seamless rhythm.

"I was sitting on the beach when human remains washed up to my feet.
The shadow of a sailor appeared in the distance. The most peculiar thing;
voices, velvet, echoed from the caves and he went inside."

Around us, seagulls leap buoyantly, eavesdropping like town gossips.

"There was a loud cracking. I watched three women carry his body out of the cave, and into the ocean.
They summoned Charon and carved out the sun tattooed on his neck."

You stare at the sky as it stares back.

"I never knew my island practiced witchcraft until the newspapers surfaced.
Two women were executed for murders dating back a decade."

It's not until we're back at your cottage
that something strikes a chord: The sun
tattooed on his neck.

"I'll make us chamomile tea, dear."

From your kitchen, your kettle hisses.
Today, it's even angrier.

The chord snaps:
How could you have seen
the tattoo was a sun
if it all took place, hours before dawn?

Emerging from the kitchen,
steaming mugs in sight, you sigh.

"Sometimes I wonder about the women who were caught.
Did they have a family? Friends?
Did they have a reason for doing what they did?
Anyways, that's enough of my old stories. How are you?"

I take the mug you offer me.

"Are you alright, dear?"

I'm not.
Behind you, a picture
I never paid attention to glares at me. It's unsettling,
like a white wall infected with mildew.

The picture is taken during a full moon
outside a coastal cave.
You're one of three women, moon pendants beaming
from your necks.

Your stories about daughters of the moon
suddenly make sense.

Winter

The initial breath of winter
always carried in
a storm.

Thunder rumbled overhead.

But it was the rattle
of raindrops
that roused them
from their slumber.

HAZARD

Dawn is approaching,
and with its melting shadows
comes the promise of rain.
The weather reminds me
of when I first heard the song
Hazard,
by Richard Marx.

Rain had drizzled all morning
and by the time the afternoon
stumbled in,

OUCH!

the clouds
were bruised
and swollen.

Dawn is a phantom
a frosty umbra
crawling
beneath room doors.

The chill reminds me
of when I first heard the news
anchor
on the television.

I sat in denial, all morning
and by the time twilight trickled in, I knew
you were never coming home.

FREE THINKER

I knew they'd be repulsed if they found out;
pass moral judgement on my actions
calling them
sinful, sordid, mad.

But what did it matter? I was liberated, not a sheep
subscribing to a set of rules.

Morality is subjective.
And besides, they hadn't felt the urges oozing
from my pores when I had kissed her.
I would never tell them that we kissed,
or that I had taken her
into my office
and had my way.

Would they call it an abuse of power?
Say that she was unable to consent?

At ninety she was hardly a child.

They could have my medical license revoked
but I didn't care.

I had to have her.
She was my favourite cadaver. I had
to have her.

Nightshade

"What is it?" he asked.

Your eyes, she answered. *They're like stars
that have lost their ability
to navigate
the souls of men.
Like that pit
where men do not return.*

FLOWERS TO ALGERNON

First date.
We locked eyes outside Clove Garden station
my second week in Aegon.

You're so tall, my first words.
Six foot four or six foot five
I remember not
now.

"Ah, an Australian! Sweet as toffee, bubbly like cham-
pagne,
she comes from down under
where there isn't much rain." A poet at noon you were,
painting compliments with smiling vowels. Heart, an open
book.

"Gorgeous smile, gorgeous eyes!"

Euphoria bubbled in my throat. Like atoms,
we formed covalent bonds sharing passions between us.
Food, physics, film,
lists went on as the waiter brought our meal. Your restaurant of choice was impressive. You'd pulled out my chair,

taken off my coat, a gentleman.

I remember coming home after the first date,
describing you to Silver as: *charming, handsome, intelligent*
and
a watered-down version of [He who shall not be named],
lighter eyes, fairer skin.
And his voice is just so deep and masculine, it is so arousing.

I remember a few months into dating,
complaining to Silver that: *He doesn't really speak my love
language.*
I liked flowers, fragrances, feminine things and: *He's sweet
but I don't want to compromise. Oh another thing: he says he
doesn't want anything serious. That means he'll always have one
foot out the door, which means I need to be ready to leave at any
time. I'm having fun on the dates but I'm not used to someone like
this.*

Silver listened patiently.
*And get this: when I asked how long his last relationship was,
he just said 'very long.' How suspiciously vague is that?
Why not just say the exact length?*

I wonder if he is hiding something.

Silver reminded me that I was here
for a good time
not a long time, and perhaps it would be nice
to venture outside my comfort zone.
Outside the kingdoms of a pampered princess,
proceeding with caution, of course.

And so, I did.

Our months together shimmered in hues of happiness.
Bookstores with basements, dinners, and galleries,
roadmap and road trips. Bee and Gee.

I was falling but
you didn't want anything serious. Over and over, you
reminded me.
Ready to leave at any moment, I had to be.
But why?
You were a fascinating book, an avid reader, as was I.
One day in the car, I asked you what the last book you
read was, and you tell me,

"It was Flowers to Algernon. I read it two years ago, just before I was released."

Oh? What do you mean? Released from where?

"From prison."

Everything fell into place.

PART II

GRAVE DELIGHTS

VET CLINIC

I work at a vet clinic.
A month ago, my co-worker, V
finally got a pet – she'd found the stray thing at a park
during her evening strolls.
Typical.
V was the vibrant, nurturing type who loved
caretaking, yet sadly had no children.

Occasionally, I'd accompany her to the pet store
where we'd purchase the essentials
cotton blankets and leather collars,
dog food for seven dollars.

Soon enough,
I started getting weekly updates on all the new tricks
she'd taught her pet. How to stand on one leg
how to drop and play dead,
how to bark on command and eat
from her hand.

Our trips to the pet store became routine.
We purchased more essentials,
a small chew toy and leather collar
more dog food for seven dollars.

Last week, the police stormed inside our clinic.
A missing toddler had been found,
chained in V's basement.

His body was almost a corpse
and the only thing on his gaunt,
scared frame, was a cotton blanket
and leather collar.
The toddler had been abducted
from a park. A month ago.

V had laughed as they arrested her,
then winked at me.
The sly thing.
She knew I had a pet of my own.

GRAVE DELIGHTS

"So," she says, staring around the restaurant, "What's one weird thing you secretly love but would never confess?"

"I'm not quite sure, it's not something I've pondered, I guess. You?"

She chews her bottom lip in contemplation. "Hmm… I suppose it's when I'm in a toilet taking a dump, and the water splashes, buns greeted with Poseidon's kiss. It's pure bliss."

His face folds. He would never agree to a blind date again.

Coup d'état

My name is Friedrich.
It means peaceful ruler,
and I was named after my father.

My father was a blond man,
with blue eyes
and hard hands
that turned red
under the South African sun.
At least, that's how I remembered him.
If you ask the people here,
they'll reduce him to a white man
with a black heart.
I'm not sure why.

He's never raped a man
or killed a weak woman
but the strangers here
still brand him a villain.

Segregation, discrimination
human violation.

We call it order.

Every Sunday my family and I
go to church and pray.
We thank the Lord that original sin
didn't stain our bodies
black.

We thank the Lord, He
carved us in His image,
the image of light
not that darkness,
that evil, which was
black.

I hate the word
almost as much as the devils
that walk around here.
All they do is weep; it's a haunting sound
like a shovel being scraped against tar.

My father always said
those who found got to keep
and those who lost had to weep.
Some called it unjust.

We call it order.

FERTILE GROUND

The widow who lives on seventy-seven
grows fresh tomatoes.
We help ourselves
when she isn't home.

They're lustrous and exquisite;
like turquoise nail polish at the beach
or long held dreams within reach.

But today, three police cars
park outside her house.
A child discovered her husband's head
rotting in the garden bed.

Seedless Grapes

I have memories of us at the bar
playing pool
your grin mixed with gin
your touch
laced with entitlement.

I have memories of me
waking up
to blood on the bed.

You'd forced yourself onto me
I castrated you instead.

Unlike you, I
always
carry protection.

CLAREMONT

I used to get a thrill
jogging by the beach;
low lights
steady steps
sudden sweats.

But since the attack
I've been terrified to walk alone
especially
during the day.
I'm afraid
one of my victims
will recognise me.

Cosmic Gas

Terror;
when you're sitting amidst
a silent crowd
and you know the fart
is going to be loud.

UNDER THE SYCAMORE TREE

I last saw my groom
on New Year's Day
with four flowers plucked
from our wedding bouquet.

Some years later
the policeman arrived
I was charged and arrested
for burying him alive.

THE MAGIC SHOP

Her ears pick up chimes of laughter
from outside but her other senses remain captive
in that threshold
between past and present.

The memory is scathing;
sweat, alcoholic aggression
oozing from pores.

Cramped corners, wet kisses
hands muffling objections.

At the sound of the man's voice
flashbacks retreat.

"I've got your results here.
I'm so sorry but they've come back positive.
You said it was your boss?"

THE INVASION

My neighbour stands
at 160cm
- redneck
- beefy hands
- pigeon chest.

The bloke's never had a car but carries a few spare tires
around his gut.

Yesterday night,
men in hooded robes arrived.

I peeked through the slits
of my window curtains:
- gagged body
dragged into a black van.

Our street was vacant.
Lifeless.

As I reached for the telephone,
one of the men lifting his body
turned around.
I froze.

Sweat slithered down my upper lip.
My heart pounded as the man's face
met mine.

Only it wasn't a man.

It was a creature with
  - horns,
  - pitch black eyes,
and a
  - stitched mouth.

The latch on my window unlocked.

THE BUBBLE BATH

We watch
the sun
spread her legs
pushing clouds away.
She's so hot.

JIMMY

We knew something was wrong
when he didn't come down
for dinner.

Then we found him in the closet
next to a dead rat.
The stench was awful.
Blood everywhere.

Was he alive?

Yeah, he was fine. But I was so proud!
It was his first catch.

THE COUNTING GAME

One stolen apparel,
two men in a quarrel
three heads
in a barrel.

THE KILLING

The rain had rinsed
the blood off her coat
the day she was forced
to slit the kid's throat.
A small white kid,
with innocent eyes.

I don't think I can,
he's just a kid!
Stop making a fuss.

But he looks so scared.
Can we please let him go?
You know our people are not like them.

Knife in her hand,
she met the kids eyes
then offered a prayer
up to the skies.

Three long minutes
and then it was done.

Remorse had rinsed
the blood off her coat
the day she was forced
to slit the kid's throat.

Quit crying my child,
it's only a goat!

The farmer's laugh bellowed like thunder.

CARAMEL SLICE

Creamy caramel
with hints of green.

Uber?

I nod. She gets in and fastens her seatbelt.
Levelling the rear view mirror, eyes
brown and putty like teabags
soaked in water.

A stranger and yet
I crave to know
what lascivious thoughts plague her mind.

Would her ego grin
if it knew of my arousing kill? Of the blood –
sorry ink – dripping
from my fingers still?

Hey... um... you missed a turn.
Creamy caramel
with hints of green —

Hello? You're going the wrong way.

— the colour of their faces
before they scream.

SPILLED INK

Now that I've forgiven you
my heart is filled with ribbons
of velvet joy.

They come in various shades;
liquorice black, frosty blue
baby pink, indigo too.
Who knew that healing could be so
c o l o u r f u l.

TRANQUILLITY

Let him go.
You'll find someone who doesn't trivialise
all the trauma you've gone through.

Someone mindful of your fragility.

For the first time in years,
I obeyed that voice
inside my heart.
I let go
and he fell
ten
stories
down.

CORRUPTION

It was a blistering morning,
the kind that promised
a humid afternoon
and a stormy night yet
her blood stayed cold
with determination.

Inside the office
smells of shoe polish and smoke
dispersed
like the clouds outside.

The officer enters
looping his thumbs through his belt loops:

Look, that man is a valuable member here.
I can grant you that restraining order...
but...
you gotta work for it
babe.

He licks his thick moustache
unaware
of the voice recorder
hidden
in her blouse.

SWEET TOOTH

"Hey kids! Want a lolly bag and a key ring?
It's a gold coin donation, money goes to charity!" says the
man.

"You can help young children just like you!"
adds the woman next to him.

They both grin but the children in the mall
continue bypassing their stall.

Then, a brother and sister stop.
They're dressed in matching bib-and-braces,
curiosity on their faces.

"Excuse me, may I make a donation please?" asks the little
girl.
Her braids are as neat as her smile.

"Yes, of course you can!"

She takes off her backpack,
fishes for a coin. "There you go, sir."

"Thank you, sweety. Here, you are. And a sweet for your brother,
just don't tell your mother."

As they walk away,
she eats the gummy bear
then hooks the key ring on her bag.

The woman's phone vibrates;
the key rings contained a GPS tracker, and the lollies, sedatives.

"How many have we now?" asks the man.

"Five. Now let's go before security starts asking questions."

THE PLANE TICKET HOME

Bedlam   chaos   a series
of unfortunate events.   Nine months
of star and sea between us and yet,   time was
inconsequential. Time never mattered   with you
time   was the moon after forever, suspended
in aeviternity, and labelled: Handle with care. Endless
memories inside.
Sunday.
In bed I lay, shedding myself through the phone, vulnera-
bility   exposed   like a new-born
naked in its cot.

I can't do this anymore.

Insides starting to rot. Frustration, grief, homesickness, all
fermenting.

So yeah, it's just too much to deal with. I'm   *I'm at
breaking point.*
"Are you saying you want to leave?"
*Yes. I'm saving up to get a ticket so I can leave
early*   *next year.*
"Early next year? That's still far away."

I know but it's the earliest I can do. I   I   sorry.
"No need to be sorry, you can cry, it's okay. And look, if it's just the ticket and clothes making you sad, then don't worry about it. I'll get it for you."
What do you mean?
"I mean I'll just get them. It doesn't make sense for you to stay longer when I have the money. How much do you need?"
Oh   wow   I appreciate the offer   but you know   I won't be able to pay you back. Don't worry about it.
"Please, don't insult me, I would be extremely offended if you try to pay me back. Take it like a gift."
Are   are   you sure?
"Of course."
I don't know   what to say   merci.
"No need to thank me. You should be enjoying yourself."
Thank you so much. I really appreciate you coming to my rescue.
"I'm happy to. It's very good to talk to you."
Yeah?
"Yeh. I get up and think about you a lot. After you gave me that letter before you left, I really thought that I would

never speak to you again and it hurt. It was painful. I kept wondering what you were doing and how you were."

Really? You know I wasn't trying to hurt you   I just wanted to tell you   all those things   I couldn't tell you   face to face.

"It's ok, I know. I'm glad you gave me that letter. It made me realise a lot of things I didn't before. How much do you need?"

I told you.

"No worries. I'll send it now, and extra so you can get a blue coat. That tiny body of yours won't survive the cold for long."

You still remember?

"That you love blue? Of course I do. I remember a lot of things. That crazy app you used to have on your phone to remind you to drink water. That time you nearly ruined your car by putting the wrong fuel inside."

Oh my gosh, I was so distracted that night.

"Yeh, I remember you are scared of a certain animal too; that time at the beach? You know what else I remember?"

What?

"Your face the very first—"

Ahh   Oh my gosh   Yeah
the fireworks   No way   That was like
four years ago.

"It was."

Wow. I'm surprised you still remember that. You're almost in your mid-thirties. Shouldn't you have Alzheimer's by now?

You were smiling through the phone.

"Well I found a grey hair a couple of months ago but not even the strongest Alzheimer's could get rid of that face."

Oh gosh   Yeah   wow   I   I still
remember it too. I was so in l–

Time never mattered   with you   time was
the year after forever,   suspended in aeviternity,
labelled: Handle with care. Sacred memories inside.

"I wish I had a photo of it."

Sorry, that was a limited edition reaction. Although   you might get a similar photo if there's ever another firework.

"Is that a way of saying you want to see another firework?"

I   Um   You know I can't answer that.
"I know."
Thank you.
"So what are you going to tell your boyfriend?"
I don't know. There's so much   inside my head.
"What do you mean?"
We had lunch and he was telling me how his friend had their
luggage stolen. He seemed so concerned and distracted.
"Everyone around him is losing things. Are you sure he's
not involved?"

There was that smile again.

Haha ha   can you imagine?   Anyway   I felt   betrayed
because when it came to me he said I was digging my heels
in the sand. But   when it came to this friend   he
suddenly had so much empathy.
"You want to say more. What is it?"
Well   he's got this other friend   from uni.   We
went to her party but I have this feeling there might be
something between them   you know?
The way she looks at him   it's like   she's waiting for her
chance. Maybe I'm wrong but   I trust my intuition.

"Me too. Sometimes it is like you are psychic. Do you think he knows?"

I don't think so.

"Hmm. Is he taking good care of you at least? Are you getting your special flowers?"

Um   He is   taking care of me, that is. But he's not like you. So, no flowers.

"What? Does he know who his girlfriend is?"

I know, you're not the first person to say that actually. But that's just because he's not like you. You're a romantic   but with actions   you get me things   you fix things He's romantic with words. And

"And?"

And   I can come to you for anything. You're always my knight in shining armour. Like this. The ticket.   I don't think he'd ever do this for me   which is fine but that's why I say he's not like you.   And he said he'd never do the distance thing. Not even try. So I don't know.

"I like it when you call me that. I am proud of you for surviving this long. It's not easy especially — wait. You said he doesn't want to try?"

Yeah. He's done the distance thing before, though. So I think it's just me. I'm sure if a girl he truly loved came along he'd try. You were willing to try for me. Sorry I'm

"No, it's okay, you can cry. I'm sorry."

I think there's something I need to do. Now. I've gotta go   but

     Thank you again   You have no idea

how much this means   I'll never forget this.

"I'm glad I could help. It's bedtime for me now. I'm in the future. Bonne nuit."

Okay. Bonne nuit.   Sweet dreams   and thank you for everything.

"Of course, you can always talk to me. You know I've always loved you. I never meant to be a jerk those years ago. I should have been there for you."

I know. It's okay, I forgave you the moment it happened.

"Au revoir."

Goodbye.

Adieu.

73

PUBLIC TRANSPORT

My bus is late again.
I'm alone at the stop,
and the rain is seeping through my clothes.
Luckily, a man arrives with an umbrella
after a few minutes.

"There's room for two under here, gorgeous.
Wanna share?" He grins at me.

I recognise him as the suspected killer
on the 'WANTED' posters circulating around.
My face goes slack
with terror.

THE TENNANT

My name is Friedrich. It means peaceful ruler and
I was named after my father. Nine months ago
my mother rented our old flat
to a university student.

Mother asked me to fix
some smoke detectors
the day the student moved in.

She seemed civilised but
boisterous and black,
I took her to be
an unreliable tenant.

However
as the summer heat settled in
I found myself warming up

to this exotic homebody.
She stayed in most nights;
curtains drawn
windows closed. Doors locked. And

as the winter fog rolled in
I found my wood

firing up
for this chocolate homebody.
I studied her from a distance, relieved

she stayed in most nights;
curtains drawn
bedroom locked.

It aroused me knowing that despite her vigilance,
she remained oblivious
to her silent entourage. Oblivious
that those smoke detectors
were my cameras, camouflaged.

CHEAT

Delicate delights.
Something magical waits in the woodlands. We walk with
a basketful of green stems
and purple petals (his favourite kind). I am seven, yes,
seven years old.

Hungry toes sink into plant matter, wet, soggy, brown.

Is that honeysuckle I smell?

"Yes! Yes, it is!" Your laugh smells hard and hollow.
Why is your face so moody and mellow?

Where is he, mother?
Why did he go away?

Face far gone you look at me and say, "I'm so sorry pet,
he's not coming back.
This is where I buried his body."

I was seven, yes, seven years old when you told me that
'disloyal dogs'
did not go to heaven.

PART III

A FIELD
OF THORNS

Dryland Salinity

I trusted you
to tread carefully
on the garden bed
of my heart.

I had hoped that memories
deep and fragrant
would blossom there.

Instead you uprooted my trust,
and planted shallow excuses.

You sowed fear and doubt
and watered down
bruises.

The salt from my eyes has become toxic.

This dry-land salinity
is corroding my sanity.

RENDEZVOUS

I met him at a charity ball
the night he stole my heart.

After a month of dating, I became enraged.
He was engaged.

No, not to be married.
Engaged
in money laundering and murder.

It's Drizzling Nostalgia Again

We met in winter
now every time a chill
races up the hill
and down my neck,
I think of her cold
feet
abandoning me
at the altar.

Moon Lake Musk

When I think of London
it's not the turbid Thames
that springs to mind
but the scent of my aunt's soap
in the hiemal mornings;
moon lake musk,
infused with tender vanilla.

I think of Battersea Park
and its f a l l e n
l e a v e s;
   merlot
     mustard
        moss.

YONDER, BEYOND OUR FOREST

We were warned
not to visit the castle
beyond the hills and valleys.
Mama told us it was the kingdom of the faeries.

She said goblins with green gums
guarded their gates.
If we went near there, they'd poke us with arrows
and feed us to sparrows.

We were warned to stay away
from the looming towers with charcoal roofs. Mama said
they were covered in flying spiders, and cats with hooves.

We were warned about all sorts of horrors
lurking beyond our forest.

But no one warned us
about the humans
who wore Crocs with socks.

REGRET DOES NOT LIVE HERE

If I had a time machine
I would go back to fourteen
years of age,
year of change
where I first met you.

The most handsome man
I ever did see
making a move on little old me.

You were a decade older,
mid-twenties
on your shoulders.

If I had a time machine
I would go back to fourteen
and not change a thing
because I know now
what I didn't know then:
I would not be tried
as an adult.

SORRENTO

Hillarys
boat harbour,
waves rolling like shoulders
in a fluid stretch.

Salt in the air
seaweed for hair,
silk breeze.

Sand
paper serviettes,
a wistful mess.
Dead helium, and
cadmium yellow
horizon stains.

JOHNNY, WALKER, JACK OR DANIEL

"There's something I have to tell you."

We pick a random table. You smell like midnight fantasy.
The air is hot and desperate (like the man playing his
banjo on stage).
Smoke twangs in the air.
I ask for a tequila, you ask for a virgin.

Sunset spreads over tabletops… mmm,
marmalade. Toast.
We toast
to the raw bun in your oven.

"There's something I have to tell you."

You don't know who the baker is.
Forget the tequila and get me a Jack.

In the Mood for Love

After much deliberation, I open my window
and let her in.
Impassioned
she grabs me by the throat
ruffles my hair
then leaves cold kisses
on my cheek.
Ah,
how I'd love the wind
if she wasn't so bleak.

SPRING

They say
that during the months of spring
old man winter
sheds his skin.

Dormant dreams
sprout from seeds,
oakmoss amber
apple green.

But I, myself
detest these months.

It's not that I hate
bearded meadows
and hairy lawns

but my nose has been
d r i p p i n g
since the break of dawn.

Cobalt skies
and bicycle bells
are punctuated
by sneezing spells.

Flowers are decorous
but you know what's not?
A bouquet of tissues
filled with snot.

THE PHRONTIST

Sleep tugs at my eyes
errands at my feet,

but to sleep before work
is admitting defeat.

So I simmer the sloth
and fire the phrontist

marshal meandering
notes of a novelist.

Now in that cranial cauldron
boiling oceans deep,

my work and my sleep
become what I reap.

MICROBIOLOGY MEMORIES

I stained him with drops of crystal dye,
exposing his chains to naked eyes.
He boasted beauty at first light,
purple pearls of pure delight!

Oh streptococcus pyogenes,
how stunning are your colonies
in all of their morphologies.

Fruit Picking

I was a fruit for your picking that night.

You peeled away
my reluctance
devoured
my succulent juices

then left me to rot
in the morning
sun.

MOURNING COATS
WITHOUT UMBRELLAS

My spirit is a tattered coat,
threads of anguish,
all unravelling.
'Be a man'

I tell myself;
loss is a language of life,
separation
a sister of strife.

Eye contact leaves me in pain.
A toddler
approaches me on the train.
Asks if I'm okay.

This time
I cannot hold it in.
"No, I've just lost custody of my daughter."

He stares out the window, and points at the rain.
"Did you forget your umbrella?"

BOUNDLESS

I used to wonder
how a limitless God
could dwell
in our limited world.
And yet,
here is my love
boundless and infinite
dwelling
inside this finite body of mine.
Truly,
I am created
in His image.

SUMMER

The sun's affection d r i z z l e d over her skin.
What a joy it was
to let the morning in.

MESHES OF A DREAM

Aqua descends
nature's splashback tiles
fracturing between banksias and flooded gum.

Sea rush.
Kangaroo paw,
why do you look so blue?

Sea rush.

You shouldn't be here,

"Neither should you."

You shouldn't be here,
it's late winter.

There stands the high flooded gum.
Raindrops ramble along its leaves.

The bark is rough and flaky
it jolts me awake.

A river stream. A pen, a puddle of drool.
A Rottweiler severing
those last threads of sleep.

CORPORATE CLIMBERS

Jack and the beans talk.
The folks in the markets
think he's inane
and perhaps
a little insane.

No one talks to beans;
they're small
insignificant
worthless.

But Jack knows
that if you want the fruits of your labour
to sprout
you've gotta deal with the beans
before their stalks come out.

STUDENT LIFE

We're out of cash
so we walk to the bank and

watch the river follow itself
through the city's canals

between bright bushes
never going astray.

ECHOES

Do we get to draw a line and say,
This is the past. Everything behind this point?
Or are we always
haunted
by echoes
of happier moments
unable to reach their source?

I'm asking
for a friend.

A Stab in the Dark

He gave me a sly smile
before raking his gaze over my body.

You know you're only
going to get hurt
right? Especially if it's your first time.

My shrug was equally playful.

Good luck trying to break me.
I'm agile
not   f r a
            g i l e.

It did hurt. Especially those first few months.
But now I'm a black belt in karate.

Autumn

Your eyes were stray autumn leaves
landing everywhere
except on me.

Roxanne

Purity has become a dirty word
now lust holds the reins
corroding the world.

MEDICAL HISTORY

I should have examined your intentions
like leukocytes
under a microscope,
and protected my heart
against your infectious
pathological
lies.

GUTS

She carried
in her belly
a responsibility
no man
could stomach.

WHISTLING IN A
QUIET PLACE

Have you ever ambled along a deserted street just as the
marigold sun
melts into the horizon, and shadows start to harden?
Around you
nightfall creeps closer; soft, steady, slow
its darkness turning branches into fingers, and lamp posts
into strangers.
Ten feet tall. Imagine

wandering through a sleepy village
and feeling as though something is heightening one of your
senses.
A chill crawls behind your neck and so
you turn around to check that you aren't being followed,
when all of a sudden you hear
whistling, whistling in a quiet place.

Years ago, I lost her to a car accident.
Months later... She returned from the other side.
But now, her aura was unfamiliar,
redolent of smoke;

not quite tangible, not quite invisible.
She was not the same;
there was a crude quality about her
that I've yet to give a name.

This story is not about a haunting.
There are no crusty castles or
demonic deceptions but I still find it daunting
to share.

It started like this:
I had chosen to drive during a storm,
despite warnings from that fortune teller,
the weatherman.

The road on which I rode was riddled with rain
and a citrus sun obscured the terrain in front of me as it shone
through the windscreen. BLINDING.
I did not see it coming. I did not see it coming
in time, I did not see the lorry
coming in time.

My memory has holes but
that sensation of escaping gravity
will I always remember.
Fragments, shattering in the sun,
glass, orange like embers as it stung my skin
and the sound of ringing, ringing, ringing.

I woke up, concussed and confused
in a hospital bed,
my neck and my head bruised and red, eyelids opening
as the doctor walked inside to give me
the heart-breaking news.

"I'm sorry. I know this is a lot to take in at once, right now.
Your GP can refer you to some psychologists
who specialise in this kind of loss.
In the meantime..."

I could read the words written on her mouth but my
ears could not detect their sound as
my pulse began to pound;
an out of control metronome beating
too fast, too sudden, too soon. Too young.

I was too young to lose her.

The doctor repeated herself, this time much slower and
louder.
Her crooked teeth were like white pebbles
scattered on a rocky beach. A tidal wave of anguish
crashed over me.
The words "accident"
"loss" and "lucky" floated around like sighs
in a meeting room. My brain could not put two and two
together.

I had her just yesterday
what on earth do you mean
she's gone forever?

I hid in my apartment those first two weeks.
No one came and no one left.
Her death had given life to sorrow
I struggled with the thought of tomorrow.

~

A year ago, I lost her in a horrific car crash
but
three months later on a winter's eve,
an occurrence
imagination could not conceive. I was heading for the
cemetery,
holding a magic charm. An old man
had told me that she could be brought back to life.
He warned me that she would not return as she was before
the accident.

Hope was the scent of wet leaves,
a canopy of silence covering me as I waited for a sign.
I remembered his instructions
as he placed the charms in a box.

"You need to listen for a whistle.
You will notice it in quiet places."

The cemetery was the quietest place I could find,
a safe space for me to bury my hopes
if this didn't work.
I opened the box, and held the charms.

Seconds passed…
and then
I heard it.
Whistling.
Whistling in a quiet place.

She was here.
Wonder beyond wisdom blossomed through my soul as
the frost in the clouds began to roll, up up
up my spine. I shivered.
Whistling in a quiet place.

Her sound was a mix between a scream
from a hollow dream
or harps in a silver stream.
Her pitch was distorted
volume slightly contorted
but I knew it was her,
knew this was the signal I'd been craving, knew she was
here.
Knew she was alive again.
I could tell that she wasn't quite the same but neither
was I.

That accident had transformed us both and

she had been resurrected, re-incarnated, regenerated.
The magic charms brought her back
now we were reunited, coupled like souls
in supernal union.
Since that evening, she has never gone away.

~

I told you that this story
was not about a haunting.
And while it had no clanking chains or spirits
I still find it daunting to write.

Have you ever gone jogging down a quiet road
just as sunset
spills its last light?
Shadows emerging soft, slow, steady,
turning rubbish into roadkill, and
bushes into beggars, hunched and haggard.
The wind starts to blow and right on cue your
hearing aids

start whistling
whistling in a quiet place.

Have you ever found yourself reading
in a dim lit room
and felt as though someone or something out of sight was
watching you. You
know you live alone, you've locked the doors inside your
home
but then
you remember that now, you wear hearing aids.
And every now and then they start whistling.
Whistling in a quiet place.

Years ago, I lost my hearing in a car accident.
I remember,
my heart and head laden with dread as the doctor
broke the news like a priest breaking a forty day fast.
I could read the words written on her mouth but my ears,
my ears,
my ears could not detect their sound as my pulse began to
pound,
an out of control metronome beating too fast,

too sudden, too soon. Too young.
Was I not too young
to experience a hearing loss of this magnitude?

The doctor repeated herself,
this time much slower and clearer.
Her eyes were a sunless sea and I felt a tidal wave of shock
ride over me.
It was so cold. Words like "permanent"
and "profound" and "sensorineural" and "loss" echoed
like sobs at a funeral but my brain refused to put two and
two together.

I had my hearing just yesterday. I'm sorry
what do you mean it's now gone forever?

My psychologist tells me that I'm going through
the five stages of grief and I've found that
personifying my hearing,
personifying the hearing loss has helped me move beyond
that stage of disbelief.
The hearing aids are a charm that can bring my hearing
back to life.

But the sound is not always the same; voices are too tinny
too deep, and when the wind blows they start whistling.
Whistling in quiet places.

The old man is my audiologist
and it was he who convinced me to see a psychologist.

There is a lot of learning that comes with wearing hearing
devices.
But now when I walk into a quiet room full of foreign faces
I tell myself this little joke.
Don't worry, they're not staring at you
because you're the only stranger in the room.
They're staring because they can all hear your hearing aids
whistling
whistling in a quiet place.

I told you that this story
was not about a haunting.
But I can assure you
that a world without sound
is just as daunting.

19 CROWNS

World-wide conversions;
hospitals became temples
where souls went to die.

BLACKOUT

There are times when I can still
feel you
moving inside me
like a gargoyle
opening its mouth
to reveal
a handful of darkness.

Au Revoir

You crossed my mind today.
It's been one year,
eleven months, eighteen days and some hours
since I (last) saw you. I remember it like a song;
we'd gone for drinks at the beach
(where we first met), to bid me adieu. Goodbye

whispered in the parking lot (where we first kissed),
a letter, folded, handed to you. Inside, years of repressed
emotions,
funnelled, into a single page.
"I wrote you this," I said, the nautical breeze bearing
witness. "I know you're not a sentimental person but I am,
and this letter has all the things I've wanted to tell you.
Please read it. It's important to me."

You smiled, kissed me on the cheek then nodded, and told
me that you (still)
had those golf balls I bought you for your birthday.
Bon voyage!

Two weeks later,
oceans and many moons between us,
I tried to start anew. Even met someone new.
A watered-down version of you,
with a posher accent.

I really tried to start anew
but that trip had laminated Europe
in memories of you.
Bone hollow phantasmagorias. Cold and sad.

You tiptoed across my mind today.
This time, I did not wince at the memories of our bodies
basking in each other's delight. *Bonne nuit.*
Instead, I greeted them with a smile. I was no longer
nineteen.
I had finally accepted things as they were;
without romanticising, or dressing you
in that hazy sweet veil
so often worn by first love.

Dear [He who shall not be named],
I feel like these poems should be dedicated to you.

You dragged my heart through a field of thorns and roses,
and in that field, I found softer parts of me; poetry. In that
field,
I mastered the art of turning thorns into flowers
sweet-scented, like lilac.

Dear [He who shall not be named],
I will remember you reading that final letter,
I will remember those fireworks from that first time.

Thank you
for chiselling me
into a midnight storyteller,
Thank you,
for these grave delights.

ABOUT THE AUTHOR

N'Gadie Roberts is a Sierra Leonean-Australian writer, creative writing workshop facilitator and orator from Perth, Western Australia. After graduating from The University of Western Australia with an honours degree in English and Cultural Studies, she spent a year in London where she started an after-school creative writing club at the school where she worked. N'Gadie is a perfume enthusiast who also enjoys watching psychological thrillers, playing table tennis, and jogging by the beach. She is currently a final-year Master of Clinical Audiology student at The University of Western Australia. Visit her at: www.ngadieroberts.com.

Milton Keynes UK
Ingram Content Group UK Ltd.
UKHW052318270224
438567UK00018B/1011

9 781922 629890